It Will
Be All
Right
in the
Morning

It Will Be All Right in the Morning

POEMS BY MICHAEL BURNS

The University of Arkansas Press

Fayetteville 1998

02   01   00   99   98   5   4   3   2   1

Designed by Liz Lester

⊖ The paper used in this publication meets the min-
imum requirements of the American National
Standard for Permanence of Paper for Printed Library
Materials Z39.48-1984.

LIBRARY OF CONGRESS
CATALOGING-IN-PUBLICATION DATA

Burns, Michael, 1953–
        It will be all right in the morning : poems / by
        Michael Burns.
                p.   cm.
        ISBN 1-55728-516-0 (alk. paper)
        I. Title.
        PS3552.U732473I82   1998
        811'.54—dc21   98-9298
                                                CIP

As always,

for Vicki,
Shannon, and Dakotah

Acknowledgments

Thanks to the editors of the following journals and anthologies in which the poems listed below first appeared, sometimes in different versions.

Alembic: "Willy Ballard" and "In Another Time"
Chariton Review: "On a Back Road to Memphis" and "The Worst of It"
Crow River: An Online Journal: "Patterning Grace" and "Elegy for Lesley"
The Laurel Review: "Looking for Frank Stanford on the Internet," "Some Answers," and "When God Met Adam and Eve for Breakfast"
New Orleans Review: "Remembering a Friend at Middle Age Who Used to Go to the Bars Alone and Dance"
The Paris Review: "General Sickles Sits for a Portrait," ".38," and "Joy's Grape"
Poets at Large: "The Lexhibitionist" and "Temenos"
This Particular Eden: "Dissembling"
Western Humanities Review: "At the Supermarket," "Ghazal," and "Winter Coats"
Yarrow: "Apology" and "For William Stafford"

I also wish to thank the National Endowment for the Arts for a fellowship I received which allowed me to write many of the poems in this book.

Contents

I

In another sky, on another night,

somebody's moon could find what mine

overlooked. All that I missed could be theirs,

and I wish them well, starting out

in another sky, on another night.

~~~~~~

William Stafford

Joy's Grape

A naked woman rides a naked man
and vamps, and moans, and both pretend to mount
the summit of desire, but they in these
small hours seem a long distance from me,
and my own passionate wave is a pain
like a volcano that has come awake
deep underneath a right back molar.
To pass the time until my next Darvon,
I write a poem in my head about a man
whose heart maybe once was like a live
volcano—but now it's harmless—and lava
that ran from his head to the tip of his toes
has solidified into that cold, hard flake
of light people see in the back of his eyes.

Soon the ache begins to grow itself
into a shape that is almost tangible,
and I don't know if it will help, but I go
get the grapes out of the refrigerator
and wash them, carry them in to the TV
in a dark green bowl. I place the roundness
of one ripe grape on top of the pain
and then, as if testing the tightness
of its skin and how much pressure it can stand
against my throbbing tooth before it splits,
I bite. It bursts. The Showtime couple arch
and bare their teeth, and somewhere far away
I feel a tremor, as if that dormant heart
were trying to remember how to explode.

Ghazal

I'd be lying if I said I'd learned from your past.
On the sills of broken windows, we're breeding dust.

Who was ever happier than when she was singing?
Blind deer follow the low notes like raindrops in the dust.

Tomorrow frozen bluejeans will hang stiff from the line.
What came in the envelope of condolences was dust.

It was only fifteen minutes away from closing,
so I swept the last customers into piles of dust.

Please, Monsignor, don't wear the fake wolf tattoo!
Congregations of the dead letter speak perfect dust.

.38

Never had a loaded, blue-black handgun
in my house, except for 1981,

sweltering summer, to be exact, way out
in the middle of America, about

two hours west of Oklahoma City
where I lived alone in some shitty

farmhouse. Fleas bit. The broken windmill
cried all night for the good young couple,

hit by a semi, who had lived there before.
Skunks speculated at the back door,

and the pool, some folk art in concrete,
was cracked and empty. I lay in moonlight

aiming my life at the stars. I hid in the barn
when cars pulled up, fired once or twice to warn

the world away. No, I didn't do that.
I went to work, and read my mail, and sat

down in a chair, next to the telephone.
I kept the gun nearby, with the safety on.

Remembering a Friend at
Middle Age Who Went to the
Bars Alone and Danced

When Stoss appeared, we didn't clear a space
to welcome him, but he made his own room
inside the crowd, moving to his own time.
He liked to twirl and swing his arms in place

until he fell, and we closed to let him stand
and sway, touching lovers as if by chance
with a shoulder or hip or wishful, empty hand.
1980. I haven't seen him since

except in the dream that woke me late last night
where I was with him. Crying, hurt,
we had climbed into a Frisco boxcar
headed out west, and we slow-danced in the door

clear across Kansas. Such music, lord,
that all of the stars put out, and no one heard.

That Winter

One frozen Saturday morning in 1972
I looked up from LPs spread across the floor
to see Kathy
(how strange to say that name
tonight and feel it on my tongue)
standing young and sleepy
in the bedroom doorway.
She had a son already
and doors already closed to her.
She said, *Take me with you.*

~~~~~~~~~

25 years later, and 2 A.M.,
Jackson Browne on a late-night tribute
sings the song I was playing then:
You'll soon be gone; it's just as well.
That's "My Opening Farewell"
from the album *Saturate Before Using.*
I remember she took my face
in her hands, and maybe
I'm drunk, but I start to cry.

~~~~~~~~~

That winter was factory nights
and fear the draft and go
to college all afternoon.
Get up in the dark
in a cold farmhouse to build the fire.

~~~~~~~~~

When she's gone, I stand at the sink
for a long time,
letting the water run.

I'm trying to remember the kitchen cabinets.
I don't think I ever opened them.

Apology

My friend, I know I should come see you,
but I'm not sure I'm one to give advice.
I almost got divorced twice
last year, wore jeans with holes in the knee,

wrote country songs.
I guess I played the fool.
If I came now, we'd probably wind up drunk
downtown, discussing

ways to trick some jewel
into coming back with us, or you'd rave
on in your misery, and I would listen, sad.
If you cried, I'd cry along.

My experience with being mad
was, just that once, believing I'd be saved
by saying, *I lied. Here's where I've really been.*
But I'm here for you, cold as the phone.

When It Was Over

Last week the storm
blew down
the wild plum in his yard.

It was half-dead
already, rotten,
but today its leaves
seem green,

and he wonders
—if he left it—
could it bloom
just one more time?

Probably not.

He'll take
the chain saw to it,
save the stump for a table.

The Worst of It

Then light and you look out.
The storm has left you dreaming about
branches heavy with wind
and rain, bent over, lashing the ground.
You had one of those nights

the day turned wrong, when it got
so still the dogs cried. The bulb you bought
for the lamp makes a humming sound.
You let her sleep.

She should be up. You ought
to touch her, clear your throat,
feeling her jerk awake beneath your hand,
but breeze blows in like blessing on a wound,
and you've known the worst of it,
so let her sleep.

On a Back Road to Memphis

This light
(the physicist on the radio
lectures, as if she, too,
were dreaming along
the highway, breathing
the smell of dead snake
and defoliant)
took 30,000 years
escaping the core
of the sun, a million more
before it started here.

She does not say
that somewhere on its way
it has fallen asleep.

As I drive on between
the fields
with the windows down,
the fist that grips
my heart is loosening.

Into this rich air
spiders parachute.
They climb to the top
of a fence and spin out
their silk, riding the wind.

2

A knowledge glimmers in the sleep of things.

~~~~~~

Howard Nemerov

Dissembling

What does this wet road running as it does
or sheen on the black limb as thin as bone,
this cloud of breath, of flame going out,
this berry growing in the barbed wire know?

My good coat's clean and hasn't lost a button.
The water's safe. I have this life, a loan.
I used to find ways not to grieve about
old promises. What is this new, fine snow?

On Tenderness, and Timing

Though they've redesigned our plates,
at first I think what I'm seeing
is one strange driver's personalized grief.
Then I look around me and find
657-CRY and 498-CRY.
The black Dodge Ram I pull up behind
with fenders like folded wings and sexy
as a woman's shoulders
says (get ready now) 321-CRY.

~~~~~~~~~~

When I heard my friend was sick
with fever, ague,
and fits of weeping when he listened to the radio
or watched the evening news,
I called to say
I was sorry, but I wanted him to know
people all over Missouri
are crying in traffic.
He told me about the clouds
of butterflies he can't drive through.

~~~~~~~~~~

I watch the new car tags, trying to gauge
how far into the alphabet
they'll be in September, when mine expire,
and I'm fresh back from ocean
and vacation, with the maples changed
and light turned hayfield gold.

123-EBB is the plate I want.

~~~~~~~~~~

Ask Me about Butterflies
reads a crybaby's bumper before me

at the stalled red light.
I've heard their pitch. They sell them
by the gross for that special moment,
giving love or death a touch of class.

I'd do it with a cage, draped
with a white cloth. When it opened,
black and yellow swallowtails
would come streaming out,
flow back into the blue.
Almost enough to make it fair to die.

Even now
butterflies ride stalks of peonies,
and over the road, fly south.
They stick in my grill and under my wiper blades.

The Lexhibitionist

When fog had cleared and sun
struck through the clouds
and I had come to work
and shut the door,
I settled into my office
with Webster's in hand,
feeling phallic, pastoral.

I'd found goldenrod
this morning along the fence,
and I'd been happy there
as I was now, reading
the words to say
what I had seen:
"yellow clusters
on stems resembling wands."

My mind drifted, but my eyes
went on across the spine
to gondola
and all the goods: tempered,
looking, humored, hearted.
I spent some time with
go-no-go, and gongorism,
then gong came crowding
in with gonadectomy
and gonorrhea.
Goof-off, goober, goo!

The summer slides.
It's going and then
gone. A weed becomes
a flower, and good faith

gets me through.
I wish when I die
to be eaten
by golden nematodes
and feed the tree
that makes the page
that bares
such words, or wave
beside the road
my wildflower
wand like any
gonzo, good-for-
nothing, good-old-boy.

Hay, Waiting

In summer, the alfalfa
in the pasture
crowds the mind,

it will not
wave in the white wind,
it lies down in the rain.

I get home
one day, and I'm
rearranged.

I used to find
the cubes a man could lift
laid out in rows

all over
the valley, but now
beyond my yard

the round bales
wait for the farm wife
to come

in her truck
and back it up
with the steel spike.

The long grains
folded green
have dreamed themselves yellow.

They hold,
like tight tongues,
what neither of us can say.

Where De Soto Met the Casqui

*—on my volunteer work at the
Parkin Archaeological Center*

I've sat flat on my butt all morning
in this July sun, digging the packed dirt
out with the sharp side of a trowel.

They gave me a *dwelling.* Where I belong
is next to the river, at the burial site,
someplace I could feel
the stirrings of the dead.

Now I'm bound
to push my luck one last time
back to the screens and spray it down:
lumps of charcoal, pieces of daub and bone.

No lost voices whisper on the wind.
Tomorrow, I'm going home.
I didn't come this far to find what's real.

Temenos

Last night the dream
I wanted to cross
to get to

a stranger who
had me convinced
she needed me

speeding
out of control
with no brakes

down the hill
between
me and deep water

took
coming awake
in a cold sweat to survive.

For William Stafford

What the river says,
that is what I say.

Nothing I find the great world
ever gave
has asked as plain

as late October leaves
this question I can't answer.
Wind grieves.

I can keep still
and walk along this road.
I can keep gathering sky,

but I want to know,
when I open my book of light,
this day gone by

the sane way water does,
or night,
in the downtown windows.

Looking for Frank Stanford
on the Internet

—a found poem

it was the road to Jericho
it was the time of roses
it was told to me
it was wisdom
it was written in the star
it wasn't a nightmare
it wasn't fair
it wasn't incomprehensible
it wasn't me
it will be all right in the morning
it will be all right on the night
it will be daybreak soon
it will be different this time
it will be good
it will be your duty
it will happen again
it will wither
it won't be flowers
it won't be long now
it won't bear mentioning
it won't do any harm
it won't get you anywhere
it works
it works in a small city
it works like this

Tending the Dead

Why has no one come
for years to tend
the overgrown graveyard
back in the field?

Mother says
*Run next door
and ask Oscar.
He's sitting up
and can talk a little.*

Two men down
the road have died
this week, and both
were younger than he is.

When I tell him my plans
to torch it,
he gives advice:
Stay out of that cemetery.
Snakes in there,
God knows what.

At 88, he sits
by his picture window
imagining the dead.
Then he says
maybe he'll ride with me
when I burn it off.

3

What life were you expecting?

~~~~~~

Philip Levine

When God Met
Adam and Eve for Breakfast

They wanted to know how much of it was true.
The dust and rib thing—stories I create.
In light of what the world is coming to,

I ought to have kicked their butts, but all I could do
was watch them move their eggs around their plates
and start at the beginning: *OK, it's true,*

I got sick as hell, and suddenly I blew
great chunks of planet. Then I sat down and ate,
in the light of what the world was coming to,

masses of shadow. This existential stew
made me so sad I built myself a mate,
then another. Long silence. Could it be true

these idiots made me jealous? *Screw!*
I said, upending the table. *It's too late*
now, I said, *for your sweet, human coup.*

In all my life, I think I never knew
such crying as theirs that morning, beyond the gate.
I didn't know what to do.
The light was bad. The whole damned world looked new.

The Old Duck Hunter Tells
One of His Favorite Stories

He wasn't the first or last Yankee clown
rejected in love, door shut on his pride,
who sailed into Norfolk and out of town
into our Dismal Swamp. To say he'd tried
to kill himself is more than I can know.
What was clear was that he'd walked all night
into the slough, as if he meant to go
too far to find. Most times they've had a fight
with a sweetheart over another lad
stealing her love, some spud with looks and swank
who makes their little poems seem pale and sad.
I've been there. I've walked that rotten plank,
so I said, *You're either crazy or lost;
get in the boat.* That kid was Robert Frost.

General Sickles Sits for a Portrait

*As a northern veteran once remarked
to me, "General Sickles can well afford
to leave a leg on that field."*

—Confederate general
James Longstreet, 1902

You've seen my tibia and fibula?
I used to take my friends to visit them
each year at the museum, septic and safe,
not the way they left the battlefield

in their tiny coffin—a joke leg saved
for history out of the butchered limbs.
I wish I had a picture of me smoking
my Havana, lying there on the stretcher.

Ignore me, dear, if I drone on, and paint
my likeness as the man I'd be: dapper
in my new coat, mustache waxed, eyes dry.
Tomorrow, early, I go to Gettysburg,

and morning long my mind's kept seeing clear
what fifty years have failed to wash away.
That day I lost a thousand men an hour.
Don't stop above the waist to show me whole.

Yes, pour the wine. Set mine in the window.
Given your painter's eye, you also see
the way light gathers and compresses time
so if we let ourselves our old lies pose

more guilt than we can swallow. After all
the dead, out of all, who would you have back?

I never loved another like the first,
an old fool says. First blood stains my hand.

My young Theresa used to wait for Key
to go into that house on Fifteenth Street
and start a fire; they'd meet in that same park
where I shot him, waving his handkerchief.

When I got old, people wanted me to tell
what I had learned. They meant from my mistakes.
They wanted me to say, *Dig In. Repent.*
Stay Calm. Be Bold. Princess, what I know

is how we ache when even our worst wounds heal.
I remember back then what I said was
This looks like a good battlefield.
I could love you. I ought to be dead by now.

Snopes Talks about Taking the Rowan Oak Tour, and Vengeance

I think one time I owned one of his books,
but I couldn't tell you what it was about.
Lots of coloreds, I remember that,
and words nobody knows, a bunch of kooks.

I'm proud to say my hometown is Jackson.
I ride over to Memphis to gamble and booze.
I'm a widower. I find a little squeeze
to sit beside, who "appreciates a man

of substance" (I laugh and pat my gut
to see she gets the joke), and before long
we're sharing kid pictures, singing that song
of better days. On this trip, the bus cut

off of the interstate for Rowan Oak.
We walked the streets of the famous writer's town
and heard the spiel, took pictures of his lawn,
and one fool stole a piece of busted brick

he found down by the stables. Outside the door
to "the study," we stood in line to pee,
and something—lord knows what—happened to me.
I felt like I'd been hit with a 2 x 4,

and all I could do was fall. When I came to,
I thought I saw old Faulkner standing there
having himself a smoke, looking me over.
You'll live, he says, *but I don't want you*

reading my books, or coming here again.
Well, you can guess how much sleep I've lost.
My name is Snopes. I don't believe in ghosts,
but I believe in history. Barns burn.

4th of July

An old friend wallows his red Thunderbird
up her washed-out drive and says he's just back
from Florida, from a drug deal gone bad.

Listen, he says, *last week these jive, wack
motherfuckers crashed in and took my money.
They held a gun to my head,* he says, *exack-*

ly like this. Grinning, he motions for her to see
what's wrapped in the blanket: a 44
Colt, long barrel. He says, *Her name is honey,*

*and later, if you're good, I'll let you hold her
and make her talk.*   *Kiss that shit goodbye,*
she says, but when they go down to the river

she likes the smoke and fire that leaps out so
it scares her some. He looks her in the eye
but he doesn't laugh. *I know,* he says. *I know.*

Moonlighting

Yeah, I think he went to hell
because he was an Indian, and we will too
because we've dug him up.
You're drunk, idiot;
help me put back the bones.
Now kill that light.
We've bought a month's vacation
here tonight, or a week's maybe,
depending on where we go.

If you'd been with me in the bootheel
last winter, when I robbed that mound
just off the river, you might be sober now.

I uncovered a child first,
buried alone, and next came a woman
with a grinding stone and beads.
Let me finish my story.
A person needs more than a drink
to face the face of darkness.

On top of the mound, in a man's grave,
I found the head pot wearing the death mask:
shut mouth, blind eyes, claw etched in the cheek.
Here was a shaman.

I did like they do
in the movies, and crossed myself,
then I got down on my knees and almost kissed him.
I remember the cows were watching.

What I Know about Gonzaga

For years I have mailed her letters
which she returns unopened,
but I have hidden outside the window
and watched her in her kitchen, holding
them like x-ray films against the light.

When I asked Gonzaga about her father,
she spat in her hand and rubbed
the tip of her boot.
I could see my face in the shine.

I have slept with the devil, she says, *and it was good.*
He's got warts like a studded rubber's
but I still didn't come.

Sshhh, I say, *people might hear you.*
Gonzaga, I say, *you must watch your tongue.*

We lay on the hardwood floor burning a candle.
She let me suckle her breast.
She helped me with the buttons on her jeans.

This morning, I saw her barefoot
in the garden, in a flowered sundress.
She was thumping the melons,
rolling them over
and rubbing their bellies.

I have kept too many of her things.
Every song I have ever loved, she sings.

I know Gonzaga set fire
to the New Bethlehem Church.
She came to me past midnight
smelling of coal oil, her eyebrows singed.

Some Answers

Why is there a need for these guns?
—Bob Edwards,
National Public Radio

Why is there a need for flowers?
—Congressman Roscoe
Bartlett, R-Md.

Because, whenever I take a hostage,
I like to have a compact, semi-automatic
flower that I can hold to my victim's throat;

because, for my trophy-head den,
I've just bought a glass-paneled case
to show off my sleekest flowers;

because, down at the wharf after dark,
I can do a brisk
flower business out of the back of my car;

because, when people pull up at my house,
full of their paranoid questions, and see a flower
poked out of a broken window, they hesitate;

but mainly because I can only
achieve, by sleeping with flowers,
a commanding, if fragile, tumescence.

Drafted, 1969

He wonders if it will wake
his parents if he turns
some music on,
and then he does, softly,
and takes down his coat
to get out a cigarette.
Turning the station dial,
lacing and tying his boots,
he practices what it will be like,
after the accident,
without his trigger finger.

He rehearses his story:
It was almost light.
I thought if I went early
I could find a place to wait,
down by the river in a grove
of hickory, for squirrels
to get out of bed, but the trail
is dangerous when you can't see
trees fallen, fences to cross.
I had a shell loaded
in case a deer should jump.
That was stupid.
I must have tried
to catch myself
as the gun went off.

Hello, he says
to himself
there in the mirror.
I'm pleased to meet you,
and he offers his good hand.

The tip of his Kool and the red band
of the radio glow in the dark.

The Ascension

Saturday, locked into the storeroom
to prepare his sermon,
he sat listening
to public radio—
a talk show gardener explaining "heeling,"
who wound and built her story,
blooming beyond hope.

Today he folds his arms on the pulpit
and stretches toward the faces beyond,
speaking in a greenhouse parable.
He says, *Lay your bodies down
into the garden of this world,
heel them in, and though
you never get back to them,
they will take root.*

What does that mean?
Doesn't he mean *spirits* instead of *bodies*?
Yesterday he knew.
Right now, his chest hurts,
and the people
in their pews below watch him sway
like a green shoot
climbing through summer's heat, groping and wavering.

The Father:
For Someone He Never Knew

Child, so real
I almost touch you,
feel
you reaching through

my fog of disbelief,
once I
forgave myself
that I didn't try

a place
with you beyond my fear,
I built your house
so near

my heart
no one would know.
Friend, sweet
daughter/son, I go

in the only way
open to me.
I say
no more than see

that you ride
in this thin rain
beside
me down

the road to home,
teenager now,
and I have become,
no matter how,

better this year.
I might wish otherwise.
You could wear
my clothes.

Willy Ballard

stands in the spread
of sawdust and blood,
having let the chain saw
snag and leap and cut
his scrawny neck,
and he holds both hands
to his throat as if
he were choking himself.
The blood shoots out
between his yellow fingers.

Now he has fallen down.

See that blue rag
he uses for a handkerchief?

Do something.

4

I know what we call it

Most of the time.

But I have my own song for it,

And sometimes, even today,

I call it beauty.

~~~~~~~

James Wright

Star Bright

When our shoulders stung from the strap of the sack,
and our fingers, shaped to the boll's shape,
were twisted pinchers;

when we'd been too long bent over,
and we stood, aching, palms pressed
to the small of our backs;

when light failed, and the red glow
came softened through a bank of evening clouds
and everyone had weighed, and was ready to go;

then we finally got to do
what we'd waited all day to do:
lie down in the half-filled wagon.

We were children. We still had faith in The Wish.
We burrowed into the cotton, beneath the chill,
and watched from there the sky for the first star.

Winter Coats

Out of this new and discount merchandise
a man appears. Our bond is what we'd have
that we can't find, it seems, at any price.
Some gray thing swallows him, and his arms wave

as if he's lost his balance. For no good reason
I say, *You must have shrunk,* and we both laugh,
and he stands watching, waiting while I put on
a chocolate suede, wired so I can't run off.

Cancer, he says. *I used to take your size;*
I've got a coat in the car that you could wear.
I measure myself. I help him tell the lie
of how good he looks. I don't have to be anywhere.

At the Supermarket

Standing in line, reading the tabloid jokes,
I'm hoping that it shows that I'm past
damned ready for this blue hair and her Cokes
and little tins of 9 Lives to get her ass

out of my lane. She and the register woman
are swapping stories of sickness. *By the way,*
she says, *I helped them bring Sister Jan*
home from the hospital yesterday.

She just lays in that bed, hurting so bad
they have to keep her doped. She likes the fall,
so we got her into a chair to go outside,
but she started screaming. Who knows what all

can happen to a person before they die?
She looks around. We just shake our heads.
She rummages for her checkbook, and I try
to appear casual, patient. Then she decides

the solution is to drag out everything:
makeup, pictures, lint, keys. She says
Ain't an old woman's purse something?
And the bag boy answers, *Every woman's is.*

Patterning Grace

—for a brain-injured child

The first time I helped, Grace fought and cried,
and I was afraid I would break her neck,
but I kept on. The second time was better.

My job was to turn her head from side to side
in time with the metronome. Julie would work
one arm and leg, W. D. the other.

She moved with us, patterning the crawl
she had somehow missed, and I could see how
we synchronized her strokes as if she swam,

right/left, heart/mind, again, toward her goal.
She doesn't know me when I see her now.
I understand. The man I might become,

touching her face, bound strength with gentleness,
as if I held the world between my hands.

Elegy For Lesley

I've lost my pulse somewhere down the road
It could be hanging off the side of the car
(My dad never taught me how to spit)

—L. A. Church, 1975–1997

Last fall, when you wouldn't get out of bed,
and I told you I'd have to give you a C,
you brought back poems on being dead

that hurt me so much I gave you an A.
What can we do in class today
with your new stuff? Some people

believe that the spark of a human soul
flies on. If you can hear what we say,
get back to work on your portfolio!

Sorry I missed goodbye at the cemetery.
I had directions, but somehow I got
stuck on the wrong side, turning in crazy

circles, wheeling, hunting a way out.
Comic. Tragic. A story I will tell.
Girl, you know what I'm talking about.

Fifth Grade

Afternoons at school
that week when she found me
in a pool of light
by the north gym wall,

trying to write a song
like you'd hear on the radio
with hands in it, and kisses,
she taught me how to fold

a true love letter
over and over
until the ends
tucked into each other,

leaving a perfect square.
This is something,
she said, *that we'll remember*
all of our lives,

but we went on to other
angles: witch's broomstick,
a pug-nosed plane,
Jacob's ladder.

Tonight when I want to tease
my daughter about her boyfriend,
I show her this trick,
but I keep getting it wrong;

something is always
left over.

Let me, she says, taking
the paper, as if
her fingers remember
the creases we folded there.

North Elementary, Dropping Off the Kids

I'm talking
fine suits
and heels, lipstick,

french braids;
jeans and big shirts,
tan feet in sandals;

women not quite
awake, hair down
and no makeup.

These mothers
grown comfortable
with their bodies

slide smooth legs
together out of the car
and stand, palms

running along
their hips.
This woman in her

short denim skirt
and retro bobby socks,
who I imagine

is rocking
just for me
across the parking lot,

turns
back at the door
and looks as if

she has heard
me say beneath
my breath: *Oh, momma.*

I Drop My Daughter Off
at the Early Morning Prayer Rally

1.

She has forgotten her coat. It's red, white, and blue.
The car radio says an icon is dead: Spiro Agnew.

2.

Suddenly I remember
my eleven-year-old brother,
with whom I shared a room,
kneeling, in his underwear,
to pray at the foot of our bed.

I was ten.
I stood there watching.
I can't swear by this time
I had given up God.

Maybe just to get this memory back
out of a morning's fog
should be enough
for me to say

I haven't yet.

In Another Time

Two doves light in the top of a snag.
We hold our breath.
My father has settled me
into his lap, the shotgun steady,
one hand under mine.

I aim and fire.
I close my eyes when the stock kicks,
opening to smoke and a deep ache
spreading inside my shoulder.

In this small moment, I'm happy
—how else can I say it—
a big boy held in my father's arms,
with him looking down, grinning.

Then, like two men
who awake together in the middle
of the floor to find they have been dancing,
we free ourselves.

We walk out to pick up the birds
blown dead beneath the tree.

Notes

"Where De Soto Met the Casqui," p. 21: There is still much debate about where sixteenth-century Spanish explorer Hernando De Soto crossed the Mississippi River. Artifacts found at Parkin, Arkansas, suggest that the Spanish spent time there, living with the Casqui Indians. The Parkin Archaeological Center invites volunteers to help each summer with their excavations, but they have yet to explore the main mound, where some believe they will find evidence that will prove De Soto himself raised a large cross atop this ceremonial mound.

"Looking for Frank Stanford on the Internet," p. 24: Frank Stanford was a remarkable poet who killed himself in 1978, when he was twenty-nine years old. I was trying to locate a copy of a documentary he had made titled "It Wasn't a Dream It Was a Flood" in the Library of Congress catalogue, so I entered the title, and this list of first lines came up on my screen. What appeared seemed to me as if it might have been written by Stanford himself.

"The Old Duck Hunter Tells One of His Favorite Stories," p. 30: The material on which this poem is based can be found in Lawrance Thompson's biography of Frost, titled *Robert Frost* (New York: Holt, Rinehart, & Winston, 1966). Frost himself gives a veiled account of the story in his late poem, "Kitty Hawk."

"General Sickles Sits for a Portrait," p. 31: When New York congressman Daniel Sickles shot and killed Philip Barton Key (the son of Francis Scott Key and the lover of Sickle's young wife, Theresa) in 1859, he became the first person in the United States to plead temporary insanity. He was acquitted. He went on to become a Union general and serve at the Battle of Gettysburg, where he lost his leg to cannonball fire. He was ninety-five when he died in 1914. Background information for the poem was taken from the book *Sickles the Incredible*, by W. A. Swanberg (New York: Scribner, 1956).

"Moonlighting," p. 35: Fifteenth-century Native American clay pots and other effigy pots like the head pot (ceremonial pots in the shape of the human head) have been discovered at archaeological sites in northern Arkansas and southeastern Missouri. Because these artifacts are beautiful and valuable, and because many of the sites where they can be found are being destroyed by agriculture, a new kind of criminal activity has developed in this area. The pot hunters often go into the remote fields and excavate the graves at night.

"What I Know about Gonzaga," p. 36: Gonzaga as a character appeared to me one morning while I was listening to a sports interview on the radio. The local coach was asked, "So, what do you know about Gonzaga?"

Michael Burns is professor of English at Southwest Missouri State University. A National Endowment for the Arts Fellowship recipient, he is the author of three previous collections of poetry. For the University of Arkansas Press, he edited *Discovery and Reminiscence: Essays on the Poetry of Mona Van Duyn* (1998). His poems have appeared in *Poetry*, the *Southern Review*, *Paris Review*, and many other journals and anthologies.